Fifty-Eight Stones

2012 Savant Poetry Anthology

Edited by Daniel S. Janik

Savant Books
Honolulu, HI, USA
2012

Published in the USA by Savant Books and Publications
2630 Kapiolani Blvd #1601
Honolulu, HI 96826
http://www.SavantBooksAndPublications.com

Printed in the USA

Edited by Daniel S. Janik
Cover Photos and Design by Daniel S. Janik

13-digit ISBN: 978-0-9852506-5-2
10 digit ISBN: 0985250658

Dedication

June Gutmanis, in her book *Pohaku - Hawaiian Stones*, recounted David Malo, one of the first Hawaiian writers, as having described fifty-eight different kinds of stones. Later works by a Hawaii authors told of their names, lives, personalities, histories, and uses. To the ancient peoples of the Polynesia, stones, like all things in the universe, had life and power. Many, like some of the poems herein, are said to have unusual powers and be inhabited by spirits. Others are just nice to have around.

- Daniel S. Janik

Table of Contents

Five Poems by Shawn P.Canon

"Bits and Peaces" is the art, poetry and music in motion of Shawn P. Canon. This journey started in 1967 in Ventura Junior College art classes, included 1967 to 1968 in U. S. Army Aviation in Viet Nam, American Hawaii Cruises 1980 to 1998, ending with San Francisco's "blues clubs" in 2000. Shawn has been a merchant mariner since 1980.

This poem was written on the last day of 1968 during my 1968-1969 campaigns in Viet Nam with the 268th U.S. Army 1st Aviation Brigade.

I dedicate this poem to my late parents, Feliciano and Betty S. Canon, my two daughters, and my five granddaughters.

Ballad of the Gree Gree Giants
Shawn P. Cannon

Sitting upon some sandbags that are situated aloft tower three, I closely watch the waves aimlessly break in a frantic and melodic pattern. While gazing at the formidable horizon with a slight onshore wink of the wind, I can see them rapidly race toward the sulked barren sands. The object of this quest is to terminate all passersby to and from the vintage gate. Good grief! Could you zing at mischievous rascals or dumb animals? However, Listen up. I hear tell that these tiny little islands are full of ghouls with fortunes of matchless box tops.

Once upon a little poem
In the land of pneumono-ultra-micro-comb
Lived a mischievous son called Chuck
Who simply had been plumb out of luck.
The trembler setting lives on
Amongst place that's outdated
'Tis called RVN, Sam's back lawn.
Now, I ask you, "Isn't war much inflated?"
Ahem! Toper heads one of the most notorious
I say that with no fictitious notion
Band, of god forsaken porpoises.
How's that for a neurotic portion?
It happened one midnight croon

Fifty-Eight Stones

I believe when Jimi Hendrix

Pierced Andy Warhol's broom

Over a julep corn mix, that's a drink I think.

The enemy approached the 13th lateral path.

The whole crew was taking a bath.

In two shakes of a lamb's tail

The good guys demolished the foe like a noon day sail.

Once againToper Dan did not fail.

- Bits & Peaces

This poem was written growing up in Waikiki in the 1960's after seeing the present day changes, but more so that I have been 'clean and sober' from alcohol and drugs since 16 August 2008.

I dedicate this poem to my parents, Feliciano and Betty S. Canon, and my five granddaughters.

Ge'me Some Recovery

Shawn P. Cannon

"What you get?" says the alcoholic addict
Acting like a macbook ipad robot.
Cautiously I look and walk further,
An onerous homeless comes up to the strip
His push cart house seems somewhat lost.

So I ponder places I have lived before
By antiquated rustic dwelling places
Along in vogue rainbow city lights
From cozy rivers by the beach
Up winding misty mountain tops
Then finally reaching 'Recovery' day by day.

Yes, I'm searching now for something
Unquestionably true and surly genuine
In picnic brunches, long walks, beach trips and mini hikes
And I say this clearly: "Could this be you?"

- Bits & Peaces

This poem was written during my 1968-1969 campaigns in Viet Nam with the 268th U.S. Army 1st Aviation Brigade.

I dedicate this poem to my late parents, Feliciano and Betty S. Canon, my two daughters, and my five granddaughters.

Kicking Up the Jams

Shawn P. Cannon

A quality of man exits within the vast realm of his goal.
Take Mississippi John Hurt, he's got 'beaucoup' soul
And the rest , well just topples the list.
I'm talking about them 'blues'
You know the kind that pulsates.
Butterfield, Cotton & Cooper reflect the same hues
Along the same frequency which may loose a yoyo jingling
miniature plates.
People talk of all sorts of power
From implements of destruction
To death's final hour.
It also includes an octopus's suction.
The only damn thing I'll die for is a heavy blues band,
Brassed and stringed on hard core land.
Yes, it'll fuse like RPG's that soar.
The populous today will never grasp the power of a
towering flower
Because they're entangled by their own hasps.
If only they would trade their twisted hearted polls for
things that will never devour
The panting beat which love passively unfolds.

- Bits & Peaces, 1968

This poem was written on a Friday the thirteenth in 1968 during my 1968-1969 campaigns in Viet Nam with the 268th U.S. Army 1st Aviation Brigade.

I dedicate this poem to my late parents, Feliciano and Betty S. Canon, my two daughters, and my five granddaughters.

Stalemate: Old and New Concepts

Shawn P. Cannon

Lo, the rustic freak who plays against the beat
Amongst oceans of musical riffs.
Do not judge our circus fleet
By what we wear.
Look at Fellini's magnanimous 'IFS'
That evolved into a creative flair.
Jimi Hendrix appears quite lame
To the small tops of antiquated jars.
'Tis a fool who cannot feel a man who played a lifer's game
By manipulating intense duels of a guitar.
Mind me, he entices any classical zeal.
You people that stand outside these progressive revolutions
Must adhere by your conscience guide,
That you, too, instilled certain permutations.
Take heed of the overshadowing entities
Of nature, meditation, music and art.
Why do people displace their anxieties
Thru implements of destruction within their hearts?

- Bits & Peaces

This poem was written growing up in Waikiki in the 1960's and seeing the changes.

I dedicate this poem to my parents, Feliciano and Betty S. Canon, and my five grand daughters.

Waikiki 2011

Shawn P. Cannon

A tired city sleeps but soon awakes us.
Many reeking homeless wander endlessly
While women asking for dates wait patiently.

A hushed street had awakened on time
By hordes of anxious sly friendly venders.
A Gold Man, a Silver Man, the Palm Readers are there
Street Minstrels and lively Hip Hop dancers too.

Yet this hectic town still glistens onward
To the harmonies and vibrant notes
Of our inspiring artistic musicians.

My pounding surf city bustles nightly here
And it puts my head in a furious spin.
Thank God daily for the Aloha Spirit
Daunting sunsets and 'dakind ono' saimin.

- Bits & Peaces

Nadia Cox

Nadia Cox is a lawyer, criminologist and poet. She lives in South Africa with her family.

Township Days
Nadia Cox

Eat masala with my hands
Blom here before time goes on
The flowers there in Mecca are baking in the sun
Calling to his pilgrims

They light all the candles
Greet everyone on the street
It's all just in your movements, the jam sticks to my soul

The way you talk is really potent
I love the kwaai expression of your silence
Bringing peace where it was hollow

Sister wants to be a social worker
We talk behind a scene of industrial villages
Sister wants to be a lawyer
She brings jasmines from the walk

Once, perhaps there was a way
A road enclosed by night and day
Everyone sees the beauty shining through but quiet hides
the pain

Fifty-Eight Stones

Maybe in October we will get purple rain
If the blossoms lose hold of illusion the fruit consequently
remains

We live in a blues outlet
Wear classic whites and jeans
He gave a walk, talk-about, and round-about
A red lift comes
We move.

Fifty-Eight Stones

Four Poems by Helen Doan

Helen Doan is a Vietnamese-American writer born in Kien Giang, Vietnam. She arrived in San Jose, California, in 1986 where she grew up. Doan self-published a book of poetry in 2002 and has been writing feature-length screenplays for ten years while keeping a journal of her independence reflected in her autobiographical novel, ON MY BEHALF (Savant 2012). Currently living and working in the county of Los Angeles, Doan aspires to make her mark on both literary and entertainment worlds.

Heartlessness

Helen Doan

Heartlessness is never old
It keeps the fearful sound
Puts her initial hunch on hold
In a flask turned upside down

To evade those cloudy days
When she grows tired of
The person her whole life awaits
One she was duly meant to love.

Her Half

Helen Doan

He knew just half the story
And oh, he knew it well
He knew one-half a story
To this warm and tragic tale

He knew her smile in the evening
Her soft and playful moods
Her scented heat, her rhythm
And eyes that saw him through

He knew better than to love her
Fanning desperately a flame
Preserving likeness of a lover
Who never felt the same

Half a story later...
The fire had since died
Still, what he wouldn't trade for
The chance to know her side!

Love

Helen Doan

Love stuns the human heart
Like a vision struck with awe
Beholding marvels far apart
Those of man or nature's law

Flooding hearts with sweeping needs
Aspirations, disarrayed
With logic tamed and impulse freed
In a massive leap of faith

Regrets

Helen Doan

Hole up in a tiny room
Put a sad song on repeat
Watch if roses ever bloom
In denial's sweet retreat

In a land of mass regrets
Of all things never said
Tightlipped silence interlaced
Woven to an empty bed

David Gemmell

David Gemmell is 41 years old and lives in the South Side of Glasgow with his partner. He has been writing for just over a year, whenever everyday life doesn't intrude. His work ranges from poetry to short stories to scripts.

For Jennifer

Inside is Where I Feel It

David Gemmell

the lingering stench
of pain and hurt
dense, suffocating.

muted shuffles along
squeaky-clean floors
into clinic k.

tunics of blue
sterilising anxiety
evaluating care.

automated eyes, scroll
health board warnings
flu jabs, quit smoking.

she sits, she waits
doctor hawthorn
two o'clock.

frightened and fragile
her name is called

steady hands please.

she's all I've got.

Five Poems by Richard Hookway

Born in Southeast England, Richard began writing poetry at school and has continued throughout his life using poetry as a place where private thoughts and ideas can be shared.

He has lived and worked in Southampton, Birmingham, and Gloucestershire as a cartographer, finished artist, and computer artist. In 1998, he left England to teach English as a second language in Portugal, Lithuania and finally Thailand, teaching at a large private Catholic School for three years before leaving to concentrate on writing.

He now combines writing and animation with teaching English to kindergarten-aged children and local college students.

For two years he had a column in "Nation Junior," the Bangkok Nation Newspaper's fortnightly education magazine, producing word games aimed at students of English.

In May 1992, he co-authored EMILY WONDERS [Harper Collins (UK) and Cutting Edge (US)] as part of their "Book Bus" reading scheme.

He lives in Thailand and has two children.

On the vocation of fatherhood in a storm.

Bay, Clown, Bannister, Quilt

Richard Hookway

Through the storm
I'll try to be a sandy bay
And offer eyes that offer love
And leave a footprint deep enough to last a life.

Through the hate
I'll try to be a clown that warms your cheeks
And draws them wider in a smile.

Through the anger
I'll try to be a banister
That keeps your feet both square
Upon the stair.
Be there both up and down.

Through the brittle spikes
I'll be the isle of quilt in infancy.
A place from where to see just how to touch the world
With all your wit and wily laughter
Till you are there in all the world
And all the world in you thereafter.

On the death of an infant.

Candle

Richard Hookway

I always thought it would see me through.
That when at last I fell asleep
The flame would still be warming my cheek with fond
kisses,
Smoothing flat my eyebrow
Keeping me bright in its memory.

But no,
And now I cannot see what to hold or turn to
And everything is black.
Just my cheek fading warm,
My eye burnt with purple spots of flickering laughter.

And though with a frantic shaking match
I can see the charred stub of what once was life,
It doesn't light again
And in time the match too fades.

Hip

Richard Hookway

When you offer your hip and the slip of your thigh
There's a catch in the air and a pulse in the eye
And the smile and the way that you unzip your boots
Is a kindling spark as the fantasy suits
And you model your shirt which shows nothing but seems
To be fresh from the cut of some architect's dreams
And your marbline neck with its marvellous 'V'
Has a dip where a nose can rest open and free
And the perfume of flowers and the muster of skin
Come together like leather and feathers and sin
And you smile at my eyes as they study too long
Like the crass adoration of icon and song
And I long for the dampness, the coolness of lip
And the powder soft hush as you offer your hip.

A personal view outlining the enormity of that which we often too simply en-label "Love"

Is

Richard Hookway

It's the breath of explosion;
The panic for air.
It's the wind-blowing, rush-racing rake of despair.

It's the seed market crush.
It's the grapple for soil.
It's the down on the ice floe, the stain in the boil.

It's the will to survive that sets teeth into flesh.
It's the will that gets roots, sheared, fighting for breath.

It's the petal's wide scream.
It's the leaf cluster's twist for the sun, for the light, for the
rain, for the mist.

It's the flatter for insects.
The battle for bees.
It's music, collision, combustion and seas.

It's the crackle of air,
The rustle of leaves,
The clear silhouetted pure space between trees.

It's the chip chop for level,
The turmoil of clouds,
The lie of the law of the jostle of crowds.

It's the grip of the grain in a splinter of wood.
It's the rot of the bad and the spring of the good
And the split of the atom,
The fury of breath as the overdose spawns desperation and death.

It's the fabulous 'fatchoo' in infatuation.
It's the lickety loose lively alliteration.

It's the buzz in the zeds in the centre of puzzle,
The catch in the throat when you do or say 'guzzle'.

It's the sting of the cold and the caking of heat
And the icing of ears and the burning of meat.

It's the breaking of wind and the clearing of throats
And the crash of the flotsam at sea as it floats

And the comfort of friends in the eye of a storm,
The exception, the shock, the predicted, the norm.

It's the wild desperation to harbour, protect,
Or the passion to penetrate, press and infect.

It's the fueling of fatherland,
Firing of faith.
It's the twisting of light that enfancies the face.

And you who insist that the bit that you name
Is the all of it, shame on you, shame on you, shame!

It is ALL!
It invented the wheel.
It discovered America, pizza and steel.

It's pulsing my thoughts now.
It's pushing my pencil,
For everything, everywhere, love is the stencil.

It's like an explosion that builds all before.
Who knows where it's going or what it is for!
But it's here and it's great if you pick up your feet
And go with the eddies, the burning, the sleet.

It's the prayers and the pondering,
The first scream of breath;
The rung after rung of the life after death.

Pretty Face

Richard Hookway

In every pretty face
I see another's heart.
I see the warmth of summer wind,
I smell the grass.
A kind of blossoming of inner love,
The inner smile,
The ease,
The orange light of journey's end
And home again.
So please
Don't mind me when I stare too long,
Too soft-eyed, too.
Because in truth I stare at someone else,
Not you.

Daniel S. Janik

Daniel S. Janik is a multi-award winning author and poet. His poetic works include FOOTPRINTS, SMILES AND LITTLE WHITE LIES (Savant 2008), THE ILLUSTRATED MIDDLE EARTH (Savant 2008), and LAST AND FINAL HARVEST (Savant 2008). His poems have been published in numerous anthologies including FIRST BREATH (Savant 2010) and WAVELENGTHS (Savant 2011) which won the London Book Festival Award for poetry. His widely-acclaimed UNLOCK THE GENIUS WITHIN (Rowman & Littlefield Education 2005) is currently in revision for a second edition. He publishes non-fiction and fiction novels under a several pen names including Gary Martine and Raymond Gaynor. His most recently published prose work, a children's book entitled A WHALE'S TALE (Savant 2009), was recently awarded a Hollywood Book Festival Award.

A personal favorites, HOT LICKS was written in Arizona during one of my *wandern*.

To my wife and beloved life companion, Setsuko Tsuchiya, who loves to travel the world together.

Hot Licks

Daniel S. Janik

Heat.

Unending heat.

The brilliance of a million flaming swords -

A million-billion flaming swords -

One

Upon a throne

Above all men.

Heat.

Dim recollections

Rising like ghosts

Above the throne

Above all men.

Heat.

Staring, one-eyed.

Heat.

"Hell," I tell the lizards.

"Life," they mimic back on

Flickering, whipcord tongues.

Doc Krinberg

Raised in California, Dr. Krinberg has worked a variety of jobs ranging from taxi driver to strip club barker before his career as a navy hardhat diver taking the author to Europe, Africa, the Caribbean, Antarctica, Persian Gulf and The Maritimes. He has lived in Asia and Hawaii, and while teaching in Japan discovered his love and need to write poetry. He has a Master's in Education from Old Dominion University and a Doctorate in Education from Argosy University, Hawaii. He is married and has four children.

For Laura

Six Haiku Triptychs
Doc Krinberg

<u>Haiku Triptych 1</u>
Pure love

Relaxing in light
Gaze piercing through sun-flecked eyes
Ice melts down my cheek

You sit still, eyes down
Face cradled easy like a child
In your hands my love

To love only once
Like each snow crystal falls soft
Leaving its one mark

<u>Haiku Triptych 2</u>
Revelry, Satisfaction, Fulfillment, Admiration

Fly you over trees
Whose tops flirt with lazy clouds
Watch I from hilltops

She pushes up high
Soaring in new azure skies
Mastering her life

I follow her eyes
Jet streams of amber, spun gold
They point to the heart

<u>Haiku Triptych 3</u>
A Wedding Vow

As the raindrops fall
so the days of our living
slip by us so quick

We lift up our hands
cupping gently the raindrops
stopping the future

In our hands float time
We gaze over the moment
turn love...infinite

<u>Haiku Triptych 4</u>
Light, Love and Shadow

My thoughts are soft hues
Like sunlight in a cat's eyes
Just daydreams of you

She conceals her love
like tiger stripes in tall grass
catlike, purrs for me

Behold, my love
Flashes across a dark sky
Chariot of hope

Haiku Triptych 5
Sexual Force...Natural and Animal

Blankets thrown away
Caught in a riptide stagger
I roll into you

Eyes and flesh pulled taut
Ears pricking, snatching sound I
Ride your tigress soul

Exposed raw and wild
In a hurricane embrace
Only for her eyes

<u>Haiku Triptych 6</u>
Disconnect, Desolate, Dreams

Whither goest thou
Who walks on the razor's edge
And sees death each side

She cries dry, tearless
Eyes hardened desolate from
Bandits of her dreams

The space between things
a dreamland not unlike the
deep slumber of dogs

Two Poems by Julie McKinney

The author is currently enjoying the life of a stay-at-home mom while caring for her three small children. She enjoys writing to encourage and educate others.

This poem describes the benefits
of fully submitting to God.

Shawn, thank you for always supporting me.

The Making of a Disciple

Julie McKinney

A year ago, I signed my name
And promised not be the same.
I wondered how He would ever use me for good
Even though His Word clearly told me He would.
A struggling Christian in a difficult place;
I felt I was always challenging God's grace.
Everyone else just knew how to live
And so they received all the love God could give.
I prayed to God for just a little aid
To help me fix some mistakes I had made.
The others just knew exactly what to do
And then there was me, who had no clue.
Where to go now? What should I do?
I needed help from someone, I just didn't know who.
I finally surrendered and admitted defeat:
All of my struggles, I could not beat.
As God rested in Heaven, I cried here on Earth
Wondering from where I would discover my worth.
Jesus saw my surrender of all in my life;
He took up my challenges and all of my strife.
He wrapped his great love around his weak little one.
"I know you only did what you thought had to be done.

I was willing to wait as long as you chose,
Now hold on to me, here is how your life goes."
I did as He said, and He worked on my heart
And created a disciple so I could then do my part.

This poem is dedicated those who feel defeated.

Mom, thanks for always being there.

The Storm Will End

Julie McKinney

The rain races down in sheets;
One drop for every tear
Shed for every dream
Whose reality will never appear.
The sky wails out with thunder;
The complaints of a broken heart.
Nothing seems to be going right.
Everything is falling apart.
But you cannot forget
That this storm will eventually end.
The clouds will clear, the sun will shine,
And to you, the sky will send
A magnificent light of encouragement
In an enormous spectral arc,
And with its color glowing strong,
The bright light will replace the dark.

Two Poems by Francis H. Powell

Born in 1961 in Reading, England Francis is, amongst other things, a poet and writer of short stories. He published three poems in the 2011 Savant poetry anthology, FIRST BREATH. He is currently working on a short story collection scheduled for release later this year by Savant.

He went to art schools and obtained degrees in painting and printmaking, working with children and young adults in London. He moved to Austria in 1995 where he taught English as a foreign language, where he continued to follow his creative muses, including music. During the nineties, he did concerts and short tours, playing electronic music. While in Austria, he began to write stories. Moving back to England, he pursued a teaching career, including teaching art and English literature and language. He moved to France at the end of 1999.

In France, he has worked as an English teacher for twelve years, and has four short stories published in magazines, including "Rat Mort," a magazine of the dark and surreal and "Freakwave." In 2006, he had numerous articles published on the internet, and started a new job, doing a monthly report on Paris' art and culture, for the "Bohemian Aesthetic." He is also a video maker.

see http://www.youtube.com/user/powellfrancis

"A Rhapsody in Summer"
is about life's different joys and pleasures

Dedicated to Stéphanie Prost

A Rhapsody in Summer

Francis H. Powell

A rhapsody in summer
The announcement of a new born child
with a perfect future mapped out.
A long wistful meander
as drops of silvery rain,
race from yielding skies
anointing our heads
nurturing our happiness.
The constellations of stars
at the wake of the night,
the planets in perfect formation.
Silvery shadows,
gilded by moonlight,
a band of troubadours
playing a masterful tune
as gypsies dance round
a fire, with flames the colour
of azurian blue.
Hands touch flesh
as soft as dolphin's fins
bodies quiver in delirious pleasure.
I walk through the eye of a storm.

Fifty-Eight Stones

I walk on burning coals,
through a pit of vipers,
a vat of oil, simmering heat,
a garland of sharpened knives.
No evil do I fear,
not one injury to report.
All is unblemished,
days span out,
like wondrous dreams.
Fires burn, throughout the night,
tenderness is shown across the minions.
All are drawn in a whirl of creativity,
fused by the lights of the stars.
Old hearts grow new
in a flurry of regeneration
as breaking waves
gently rumble, close to the shore.
Good news is passed on by Mercury himself,
while bathing in an ocean of crystalline lather.
Conversations are laced with splatters of good will
humor and empathy and witty refrain.
All of this as we wander our way home,
such bliss and pleasure in our hands to keep.
The spiral, the vortex,
the Tibetan bell
all sing like a celestial choir

as trinkets drop gently from the skies
landing in the hands of the needy.
No need to rummage for food
as all is of plenty.
Oh if this day could come today
We could all walk so tall and proud
and share in the life of the gods.

Inspired by topical events. "The Raven" is a dark prophecy.
about the corruption rife in this world.

Dedicated to Stéphanie Prost

The Raven - Part 1

Francis H. Powell

The raven circles closer
It's spreading wings
cast a deep shadow,
on a world cowering below
The metronome gives
out a jittery sinuous measure
from which there is no respite,
I look on in bewilderment
drawn by the vector of
a temple dedicated to greed
fabricated by a more fearsome
reincarnation of Loki himself
where men in spandex suits,
dressed up like pimps
on a bumper pay day
all to the nines,
with pockets bulging with plunder
in their bloated pantaloons
all bovine faces
and double chins concertinaing
like a deflated helium balloon
and complexions, the colors of blood diamonds

glibly plunge a needle
deeper than deep
into a fleshy welcoming arm
injecting another toxic dose of
vulgar undiluted corruption,
while the money, drips, drops, drips
into a well of euphoric extravagance
They will catch up with you ,
as sure as night and day
You'll be clamped, pinioned and snared
by a leg,
by a toe,
by any follicle,
discernable on your gangling frame
wrenched by an ear,
while swarming the sanctity
of your cerebellum,
bungling brain-parts
catching you painfully off guard
exploiting the chinks in your apathy
in dot com scams,
hacking scamduggery
fashioned on some flat screen
a bitmonkey's computadora
playing trickery on your coffers
Pulling at the very hair attached to

the warm bed that is your skull
Hoovering up your last scrap of self-esteem
While you meekly protest,
flailing arms in the air
or plucking at the petals of a flower called despair
screaming with a voice as hollow as
solitude itself.
Those dream busters never refrain,
from scratching away at that last morsel of dignity
that has sustained you over the passing years
like the last candle left burning, after a tempest
no hiatus to draw breath
parked at your doorstep
an overt show of harassment
Lodged in readiness
are these gallery of rogues,
like kamikazes on a one way trip to oblivion
the road is never long enough
further than Antioch you must go
to find cover, as they trail your shadow
with the eagerness of a headhunter
tracking a prize convict, back from a Roman holiday
It's the Eleusinian way to travail to
the afterlife, clinging to
a promise that can only be
dreamt up by ancients, screaming for immortality

In the last adorned vestiges of hope
As their last breaths and contemplation
compete with the shrill sound of
cats being stroked by the talons of hawks
While Joe six-pack is caked out on cactus nectar
masquerading down, the washed up on the shores of
delusion
As a vast trail of trunked up turbines,
built on sand-dust fairies'
shavings are both mind blowing
mean and monstrous
Chomping up the land
morsel by morsel
While shouting out outdated dogma
Watch those sledgehammering slingers
dig deep into the pits
which are clogged up with
black honey spewed
from the hives of hades.
Oh my jiggaboo Jesus,
we could never be late for church,
for to be late was like missing an appointment
with a shizzle dang shrink
who might with withhold the keys to eternity, while
redirecting the unholy to a third rate hotel.

The Raven - Part 2

Francis H. Powell

I stand before, a construction built of malformed
molecules,
on foundations of a crust of bread,
wrenched from the mouth of a beach bum,
strung out on the wine sieved by Bacchus and Dionysus,
through a fuzzy wooly network of titanium floss,
in a virtual jumped up swirly gig
as thick as modified molecular molasses
But the music was strum fink dumb
And the priest seemed to be blind to the echoes of war
He was a naïve Nirvana
that never drummed up a beat,
in this two tone periphery
His cloth as gray as a sky over Cherrapunji
As incense knew no boundaries, rasping the nostrils,
like a whirl storm of curry powder
Filling my head with hydrogen dreams
that went up to the clouds and back
on some cosmic voyage
accompanied by Hermes, no less
safe from harlots and crones
attested and sure, no hullaballoo hysterics

so to speak

While prisoners with pork pie hats preached sermons

that would only make sense

to a seventeenth century psi-boner

not far from the radar of uncertainty.

The ash cloud hovers,

released from the shackles of its dormant repose

as dense as the aroma of a Hiawatha peace pipe

The head of the IMF is cuffed

His cranium cursing the world of chambermaids

and their enticing frocks,

blacker than rook's feathers

Ignobility laid bare,

as a lizard grasping to a leaf

as thunderclouds shatter

His ashen gray face,

as deflated as a Zeppelin,

stabbed with a scalpel

even an ice cream

with sprinklings of heavenly sherbet

couldn't elevate his spirits

that drone and throb

like the electricity in an abattoir

and there is nothing that can stop

the waves of the ocean growing in force

reaching upwards like

Stronmaus , awoken from a slumber
covering the lowlands
Those thin strips of land,
so vulnerable and exposed
to the whims of nature
as the earth's crust recoils, rattled by the
cumbersome tread of
The Jinshin-Mushi, of mythical repute
who pound their fists on the ground
in a chorus of descent
Feasting on mankind's fallibility
Like a rag doll clenched and churned
in the mouth of a salivating wolf
buildings crudely topple over
transforming into dusty powdery cloud clusters
as if the sky had crumbled down to earth
While the last remaining picture
of an enigma, the much vilified bearded man,
with eyes as soft as koala bear's,
but a wanton mind as destructive and
as a flame thrower in a paper mill,
is painted through the helmet of
a non-descript marine,
the dragon slayer, the faceless bounty hunter
with the charge of
plugging holes in the notorious one's head,

to eliminate his symbolic allure
As woman wail, the vision is relayed to control center
far in the bunker of clandestine reclusedom
a sanctuary, as dimly lit as a bat's cave
The wounds are as big as squashed tomatoes
as red as genetically modified geraniums
to disturbing to broadcast, or so they said
They might upset the world's delicate equilibrium
Then his body is slung, with great precision
deep into an ocean of questions and
acrimony, to bosom of invisibility
with the sound of a military toot
and a prayer of unheard laments.
Lost forever, less the relics of latent curiosity
Different facets of the truth are concocted
and then re-concocted
relayed by smooth skinned fresh college boys
All of the facebook generation , weaned on
doughnuts, reality TV, and shifting spin doctor jive,
As the legend of the infamous housebound prisoner
caught in the belly of a palatial compound
is now revenged.

The Raven - Part 3

Francis H. Powell

A decade's debt now repaid,
in some kind of swift atonement
the chapter closed the book slammed shut,
with the thud of a hydrogen bomb
going off in a dense metropolis
The news breaks to the cheer
of many, spaced out on Starbucked latte dreams,
Caught on a blackberry,
Or an internet intravenous
A cyberpad is a tablet,
mandatory for the modern day voyager,
like a map was to weatherworn seadog
News spreads quicker than the eye of a tornado
Veiled is the specter of a nuclear cloud
spewed out from the eastern shores
spreading itself like an unwelcome
inebriated guest at a Mormon wedding fest
Spiraling, and beating a path of destruction
In a giddy dance
an atmospheric cataclysmic catastrophy
Chernobyl reignites in the mind
While Fukushima marks a new installment

for those who'd forgotten
how the original story had unfolded
fused by the folly of greed
and bulging bank accounts,
swelling with geld
the owners of which are unabashed
Jiving to the Rat ta tat tat of
elasticated accountant tapped numbers
mulled on a cash-cow lifestyle
as we the enslaved ones
the fodder, the dunderheaded crew
The obedient sheep that follow
the endless line, only working, to make the rich richer
doing our prosaic meaningless jobs
as the cattle truck speeds on to Armageddon
The warlords still sell their wares
As many new wars are contrived
to fit around TV schedules
To be remade into funked up cinematic action movies
for popcorn junky teens,
spawned on computer games,
and the configurations of the latest Manga delights
that corrode what were once pure minds
As Machu Picchu once loomed tall, over the horizon
The prince of the Grigori swishes his tail
and seeds now fall on barren land

singed with gusts of bile
and the air is spiked with pestilence
Wave after wave
Spewed remorselessly
The land heaped with slag
Choke we do
Asthmatics annihilated
All respirator recluses
Poverty is stamped with a chaste kiss
as sweet as a contaminated field of tulips
Many living cardboard crusted townships
with only scraps to fight for
Their cries dismissed, plastered over,
by the veneer of more palatable visions,
more serene, less tiresome intrusions
The Vatican shimmies on, in golden splendor
The holy one sits majestically
on his pile of trinkets,
a scepter cradled in his grip
a crown of duty rests on his bonce
his every need tended for
Cleopatra's bathwater still permeating
bicarbonate soda and salt in a quart of water.
melted honey swills in milk.
kept to a perfect temperature
the thermostat on hold

Fifty-Eight Stones

A bed of duck plumes that molds
around his rotund form
His mutton, enriched by a fine profuse gravy
While his belly lies full,
his thoughts are enmeshed
in spiritual arcadia
floating high above mortals torments
His clothes so clean and white,
gilded with the insignia of his office
blinding in perfection
soft as dandelion parachutes.

The Raven - Part 4
Francis H. Powell

The Vatican laundry so *efficiente*
A million miles from the slums of Mumbai
Where children dwell in strictly putrid abodes
Stacks of rubbish offer measly shelter
Never living off the land of plenty
only toxin air to respire
no water swelling from the foothills of the Himalayas
Their heads tired from dreams that will never see light of
day
legions of rodents jostle in sharp configuration
Begging's the only likely pathway to sustenance
Too far away, to touch us, their voices never reach our ears
not even nudges of deprivation
in our own neighborhood, hold sway
As we are lain in our comfortable divans,
tucked away in the guard of angel's wings
closeted while bereft of worries
But a smart phone, is no remedy in the deep pits of the
poverty trap
on the long dusty road to Damascus
As the chase for the dirty dollar
gathers wanderlust

Fifty-Eight Stones

The sullied yen's sun
dips below the horizon
rattled by misfortune.
The soiled up pound
is in the Eaton boy's domain
As he rapaciously goes about
tearing up the social fabric
"Close down that library,
poor people don't need to read books,
or wonder at Shakespeare's
rhymes, meters and stanza,"
he screams to a trusty subordinate
as the ruler's edict, stabs another wound in
an unshielded heart
There is no place left at the last supper
The table has already been laid
and don't come a banging on the door
the porthole blocked by heavy steel girders of restraint,
that could keep out a marauding army, at bay
where impenetrable exclusivity holds sway,
While banker's bonuses sing out
louder than a choir from hell
and the world sings to the tune
of corporations' ugly tenure
more powerful than dominions
of the past, and more puissant than many

in the present climes
As Usain Bolt spikes serendipity
Kismet karma conundrum questions
are muttered out of marijuana
clustered mouths, searching for refuge
In tenements daubed in gooji gaji graffiti
Corrupt venal regimes continue to clatter
vanity sustains their onward journeys
With a perpetual power-lust squall in their sails
their hands dipping, in the coffers of state
these weasel-worded warmongers
all members of the most heinous of tribes
plotting one last apocalyptic shebang
are happily ensconced
in corrupt regime holiday homes
at their Svengali's expense
filled with gewgaws and spoils
Their Megadomah creeping shadows
Jangle louder than an orchestral megadeath
The raven swoops lower
I can feel its stinging breath on my face

Four Poems by Jean Yamasaki Toyama

Jean Yamasaki Toyama is professor emerita of French at the University of Hawaii, Manoa and former Associate Dean of the College of Languages, Linguistics and Literatures. Her recently published work includes *No Choice but to Follow,* written with Juliet Kono, Christy Passion and Ann Inoshita and Kelli's Hanauma Friends. Her poems were included in the internatiionally- awarded anthology, WAVELENGTHS (Savant 2011).

Ambition

Jean Yamasaki Toyama

it is perhaps to silence
that I should aspire
instead of succumbing like a coward
to the temptation of words
which in their seduction
pitch high in siren sounds

my silence should be my seal

Antiphonal

Jean Yamasaki Toyama

Give us life that decays with time
give us the ecstasy of perishing.

- Ooka Makoto

If it could come in one fucking end
that we crave, pursue and obsess over,
then our decay over time would not
leave us so dumbfounded that
all we do is avoid, or think we
avoid, the relentless crumbling
of our edifice.

Footfalls

Jean Yamasaki Toyama

I heard his footsteps right behind me
not a running pace, more a sly saunter,
deliberate, distinct.
So I quickened my step, not much, just a little.
I was not scared,
but that footfall echoed
a cadence as fast as mine.
This went on for a while, slow, quick,
slow, quick, quick, like some
dance step:
slow, quick and slow.
I could not lose him.

Then the years went by
he drew nearer as I slowed down
quick or slow
whichever pace could not distract him;
then he was beside me.

He never leaves me now. Soon
we'll go together.

Heroes

Jean Yamasaki Toyama

How do they do it?
Those who shoot sweet little girls and
tired old women running in panic.

How do they do it?
Those who disembowel plump newborns
and muscle men split open by bullets.

How do they do it?
Those who aim in their sights ragged adolescents,
perfumed newlyweds, lean old men, and three-legged dogs.

How do they do it?
Eat. Sleep. Love.

How they do dream!

Five Poems by Vivekanand Jha

Vivekanand is a translator, editor and award winning poet from India. He holds a Diploma in Electronics and Communication Engineering, a Certificate in Computer Hardware and Networking, and both MA and PhD in English from Lalit Narayan Mithila University Darbhanga. He is a contributing poet to WAVELENGTHS (Savant, 2011) which won first place in the 2011 London Book Festival. He is Poetry Contest Winner-Third for his poem "Hands Heave to Harm and Hamper" in Beginners®, a documentary, graphic, nonfiction book series. He has authored five books of poetry, including one critical book on the poetry of Jayanta Mahapatra, as well as edited two critical anthologies on Indian English Writing.

His writings have been published in more than sixty magazines round the world. His poems have been published in more than fifteen poetry anthologies. He has more than twenty research and critical articles published in various national and international anthologies and refereed journals. He is son of noted professor, poet and award winning translator Dr. Rajanand Jha (Crowned with Sahitya Akademi Award, New Delhi).

Flogging a Dead Horse
Vivekanand Jha

Ah, widow!
You have never been a civil citizen
always mutilated from constitution
like forbidden and fanatic institution.

Not for you fundamental rights
Not for you democratic exercise
These are of the men,
for the men and by the men.

You are simply an institution
To mull over sorrows, agonies and pains.

Not for you these finger licking flavours
What to tell of meet, mutton, chicken or fish
Not for you even garlic, onion and spice:
That may arouse in you other hunger to quench;
That may set in you an anger to retaliate.

Because they want you
to be a deserted visitation and stone
where one could spit full of mouth

and piss full of bladder.

They want you to be a bleak destination
Where they could discharge
Their reverberating and brazen passion
And you couldn't loud an assault in defense.

They do all for their own want
But nothing for the want of you.

Fool

Vivekanand Jha

He can be without food, not without folly
Sitting in silence he is supposedly a scholar
All he needs is to open his mouth only once
There begins all the glory of his idiocy:

Words he spat stinking and reeking like
Rotten eggs and decayed carcass
The doctrine he defines, unfolds tragedies
Not of less magnitude than
Tsunami, quake or nuclear explosion
The name he is baptized
is not less than a legendary figure.

It's not too difficult to single him out
Positioning blatantly in the huge crowds
He begins, when all else finish their laughing,
He applauds, when all else end their clapping,
He cuts only those trees leaning towards him
He smacks the flies sitting over his face.

Multicolor
Vivekanand Jha

All things bad and beautiful
brimming with colour clueful.

Colour of success, at risk to faint
if it falls in the hands of tyrant.

Colour of love has lightning lusture
like animal has after grazing pasture.

Colour of confidence care for none,
success for him like for a lady a bun.

Colour of money has peculiar chemistry,
even dead comes out of cemetery.

Colour of words has magical feature.
even fools pretend to be a scholar.

Song of Yoga
Vivekanand Jha

Observe once a day meditation
Achieve mental clarity-concentration.

Feel fit-fine even in confinement
Improve your posture-alignment.

Keep your mind youthful-supple
Cven without running- double.

Inhale oxygen profuse but slow
Brings on face freshness and glow.

It bolsters and builds brain
By combating stress and strain.

Attain a deeper level of relaxation
Deeds of heroic do in fraction.

Solemnize marriage of mind-body-spirit
And stand in a state of eternal bliss.

Yoga, free and priceless panacea,
Given away by celestial ambrosia.

Spider
Vivekanand Jha

As spider tosses his own web
Everyman in his own-carved cave
Where he himself a creator,
himself a destroyer
Where he himself the president,
 himself a servant.

Like woes and widow,
Like light and shadow,
Like destitution and prostitution,
Gay and lesbian go together.

Now he is straight, now he is gay
Now he is a plebian, now he is a lesbian
Now inside door, now on road
Now in street, now on broad
God makes one, man makes many.

If you enjoyed *Fifty-Eight Stones: 2012 Savant Anthology of Poems*, consider the first in the series, *First Breath: 2010 Savant Anthology of Poems*

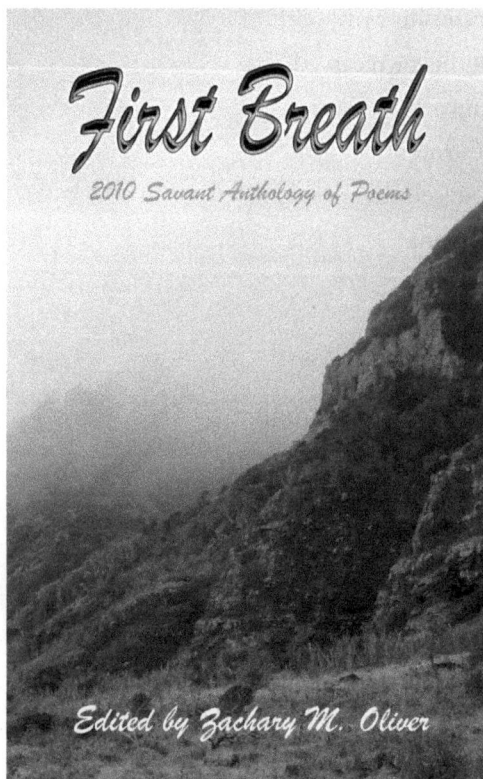

Twenty-nine poems by ten outstanding poets and writers selected for their outstanding merit including Helen Doan, Erin L. George, Jack Howard, Daniel S. Janik, Scott Mastro, Zachary M. Oliver, Francis H. Powell, Gabjirel Ra, V. Bright Saigal and Orest Stocco

And the London Book Festival award-winning poetry anthology, *Wavelengths: 2011 Savant Anthology of Poems* (Savant 2012):

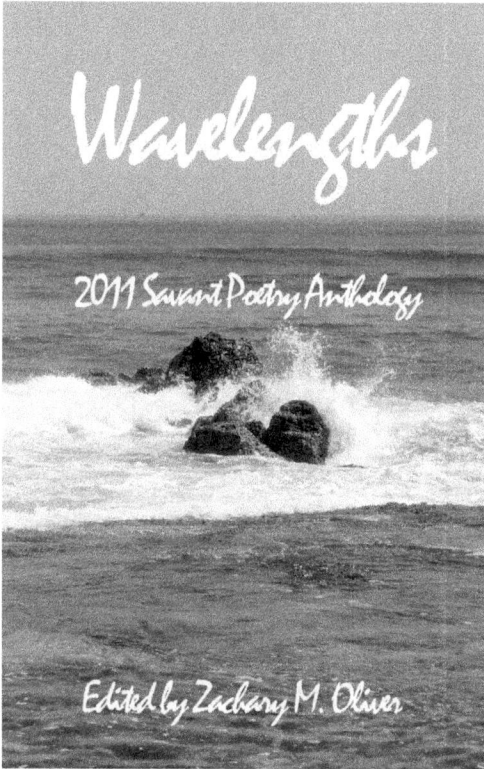

Thirty-eight poems by sixteen outstanding poets including Penny Lynn Cates, J. R. Coleman, Nadia Cox, Helen Doan, Four Arrows, Erin L George, IKO, Daniel S. Janik, Vivekanand Jha, Alex Kelley, Zachary M. Oliver, Cara Richardson, Michael Shorb, Jason Sturner, Jean Yamasaki Toyama and Jeremy Ussher.

Also, consider these other fine books from Savant Books and Publications:

Other Savant Poetry Books:
First Breath Edited by Zachary M. Oliver
Last and Final Harvest by Daniel S. Janik
The Illustrated Middle Earth by Daniel S. Janik
Footprints, Smiles and Little White Lies by Daniel S. Janik

Other Savant Books by These Poets:
A Whale's Tale by Daniel S. Janik
On My Behalf by Helen Doan
Flight of Destiny by Francis Powell (soon to be released)

Other Savant Books, CDs, DVDs:
A Whale's Tale by Daniel S. Janik
Tropic of California by R. Page Kaufman
Tropic of California (the companion music CD) by R. Page Kaufman
The Village Curtain by Tony Tame
Dare to Love in Oz by William Maltese
The Interzone by Tatsuyuki Kobayashi
Today I Am a Man by Larry Rodness
The Bahrain Conspiracy by Bentley Gates
Called Home by Gloria Schumann
Kanaka Blues by Mike Farris
First Breath edited by Z. M. Oliver
Poor Rich by Jean Blasiar
The Jumper Chronicles - Quest for Merlin's Map by W. C. Peever
William Maltese's Flicker by William Maltese
My Unborn Child by Orest Stocco
Last Song of the Whales by Four Arrows
Perilous Panacea by Ronald Klueh
Falling but Fulfilled by Zachary M. Oliver
Mythical Voyage by Robin Ymer
Hello, Norma Jean by Sue Dolleris
Richer by Jean Blasiar
Manifest Intent by Mike Farris

Charlie No Face by David B. Seaburn
Number One Bestseller by Brian Morley
My Two Wives and Three Husbands by S. Stanley Gordon
In Dire Straits by Jim Currie
Wretched Land by Mila Komarnisky
Chan Kim by Ilan Herman
Who's Killing All the Lawyers? by A. G. Hayes
Ammon's Horn by G. Amati
Wavelengths edited by Zachary M. Oliver
Almost Paradise by Laurie Hanan
Communion by Jean Blasiar and Jonathan Marcantoni
The Oil Man by Leon Puissegur
Random Views of Asia from the Mid-Pacific by William E. Sharp
The Isla Vista Crucible by Reilly Ridgell
Blood Money by Scott Mastro
In the Himalayan Nights by Anoop Chandola
Rules of Privilege by Mike Farris
On My Behalf by Helen Doan

Soon to be Released:
Light Surfer by David Allan Williams
Perverse by Larry Rodness
Traveler's Rest by Jonathan Marcantoni
Keys in the River by Tendai Mwanaka
The Juper Chronicles - *Path of the Templar* by W. C. Peever
The Loons by Sue Dolleris
The Judas List by A. G. Hayes

http://www.savantbooksandpublications.com